THANKFUL, BLESSED &
SOMETIMES STRESSED

THANKFUL, BLESSED & SOMETIMES STRESSED

PRAYER JOURNAL

RENEE SPIVEY

Tymm Publishing

Paperback ISBN: 978-0-9990469-2-0

Publishing Assistance: Tymm Publishing LLC
Cover and Book Design: Tywebbin Creations LLC
Editing: Felicia Murrell

CONTENTS

INTRODUCTION

Sometimes prayer can be a difficult task. We struggle to find the right words to say. Outside influences interrupt us, and our thoughts become jumbled. At least for me, I found that to be true.

When I write my prayers down, the words seem to flow more smoothly and I express myself more clearly. I don't have to worry about people criticizing me for not saying the perfect prayer, using improper grammar or any of the other myriad of things we tend to criticize.

I have created this journal with simple prompts to assist you in writing your prayers. In Psalm 142:2, David declares, "I pour out before Him my complaint; before him I tell my trouble." May your words flow freely and the meditation of your heart be clear as you write out your prayers on the following pages.

It is my prayer that this journal will be an effective tool in your prayer life, and that by the time you reach the last page of this journal, you can look back over your requests and see answers to those prayers.

Always remember, "The prayer of a righteous person is powerful and effective."

DATE: _____

PRAYER PROMPT – GIVE THANKS…

_____

_____

_____

_____

_____

_____

_____

_____

_____

_____

_____

_____

_____

_____

_____

_____

_____

_____

_____

"This is the day the Lord has made; We will rejoice and be glad in it." ~ Psalm 118:24

_____

_____

_____

_____

_____

_____

_____

_____

_____

_____

_____

_____

_____

_____

_____

_____

_____

_____

_____

_____

"This is the day the Lord has made; We will rejoice and be glad in it." ~ Psalm 118:24

DATE: _____

PRAYER PROMPT – SAY YES...

_____

_____

_____

_____

_____

_____

_____

_____

_____

_____

_____

_____

_____

_____

_____

_____

_____

_____

_____

_____

_____

"Rejoice always, pray continually, give thanks in all circumstances; for this is God's will for you in Christ Jesus." ~ 1 Thessalonians 5:16–18

_____

_____

_____

_____

_____

_____

_____

_____

_____

_____

_____

_____

_____

_____

_____

_____

_____

_____

_____

_____

_____

_____

_____

"Rejoice always, pray continually, give thanks in all circumstances; for this is God's will for you in Christ Jesus." ~ 1 Thessalonians 5:16-18

PRAYER PROMPT – REVIVE ME AGAIN…

_____

_____

_____

_____

_____

_____

_____

_____

_____

_____

_____

_____

_____

_____

_____

_____

_____

_____

_____

_____

"This is the confidence we have in approaching God: that if we ask anything according to His will, he hears us." ~ 1 John 5:14

_____

_____

_____

_____

_____

_____

_____

_____

_____

_____

_____

_____

_____

_____

_____

_____

_____

_____

_____

_____

"This is the confidence we have in approaching God: that if we ask anything according to His will, he hears us." ~ 1 John 5:14

DATE: _____

PRAYER PROMPT – IT'S SO HARD…

_____

_____

_____

_____

_____

_____

_____

_____

_____

_____

_____

_____

_____

_____

_____

_____

_____

_____

_____

"Devote yourselves to prayer, being watchful and thankful." ~ Colossians 4:2

_____

_____

_____

_____

_____

_____

_____

_____

_____

_____

_____

_____

_____

_____

_____

_____

_____

_____

_____

_____

_____

_____

"Devote yourselves to prayer, being watchful and thankful." ~ Colossians 4:2

DATE: _____

PRAYER PROMPT – MOMENTS OF DOUBT…

_____

_____

_____

_____

_____

_____

_____

_____

_____

_____

_____

_____

_____

_____

_____

_____

_____

_____

_____

"Do not be anxious about anything, but in every situation, by prayer and petition, with thanksgiving, present your requests to God." ~ Philippians 4:6

_____

_____

_____

_____

_____

_____

_____

_____

_____

_____

_____

_____

_____

_____

_____

_____

_____

_____

_____

"Do not be anxious about anything, but in every situation, by prayer and petition, with thanksgiving, present your requests to God." ~ Philippians 4:6

DATE: _____

PRAYER PROMPT – SEASONS OF LIFE...

_____

_____

_____

_____

_____

_____

_____

_____

_____

_____

_____

_____

_____

_____

_____

_____

_____

"Therefore I tell you, whatever you ask for in prayer, believe that you have received it, and it will be yours." ~ Mark 11:24

_____

_____

_____

_____

_____

_____

_____

_____

_____

_____

_____

_____

_____

_____

_____

_____

_____

_____

_____

"Therefore I tell you, whatever you ask for in prayer, believe that you have received it, and it will be yours." ~ Mark 11:24

DATE: _____

PRAYER PROMPT – WHAT'S HOLDING YOU BACK?

_____

_____

_____

_____

_____

_____

_____

_____

_____

_____

_____

_____

_____

_____

_____

_____

_____

_____

_____

"Then you will call on me and come and pray to me, and I will listen to you."
~ Jeremiah 29:12

_____

_____

_____

_____

_____

_____

_____

_____

_____

_____

_____

_____

_____

_____

_____

_____

_____

_____

_____

_____

_____

"Then you will call on me and come and pray to me, and I will listen to you."
~ Jeremiah 29:12

DATE: _____

PRAYER PROMPT – PRACTICE WHAT YOU PREACH…

_____

_____

_____

_____

_____

_____

_____

_____

_____

_____

_____

_____

_____

_____

_____

_____

_____

_____

_____

"Be joyful in hope, patient in affliction, faithful in prayer." ~ Romans 12:12

_____

_____

_____

_____

_____

_____

_____

_____

_____

_____

_____

_____

_____

_____

_____

_____

_____

_____

_____

_____

"Be joyful in hope, patient in affliction, faithful in prayer." ~ Romans 12:12

DATE: _____

PRAYER PROMPT – WHEN IT'S HARD TO HAVE FAITH…

_____

_____

_____

_____

_____

_____

_____

_____

_____

_____

_____

_____

_____

_____

_____

_____

_____

_____

"Let us then approach God's throne of grace with confidence, so that we may receive mercy and find grace to help us in our time of need." ~ Hebrews 4:16

_____

_____

_____

_____

_____

_____

_____

_____

_____

_____

_____

_____

_____

_____

_____

_____

_____

_____

_____

"Let us then approach God's throne of grace with confidence, so that we may receive mercy and find grace to help us in our time of need." ~ Hebrews 4:16

PRAYER PROMPT – WILL IT EVER STOP?

_____

_____

_____

_____

_____

_____

_____

_____

_____

_____

_____

_____

_____

_____

_____

_____

_____

_____

_____

"But when you pray, go into your room, close the door and pray to your Father, who is unseen. Then your Father, who sees what is done in secret, will reward you." ~ Matthew 6:6

"But when you pray, go into your room, close the door and pray to your Father, who is unseen. Then your Father, who sees what is done in secret, will reward you." ~ Matthew 6:6

PRAYER PROMPT – I'M TIRED OF CRYING…

_____

_____

_____

_____

_____

_____

_____

_____

_____

_____

_____

_____

_____

_____

_____

_____

_____

_____

"But when you ask, you must believe and not doubt, because the one who doubts is like a wave of the sea, blown and tossed by the wind." ~ James 1:6

_____

_____

_____

_____

_____

_____

_____

_____

_____

_____

_____

_____

_____

_____

_____

_____

_____

_____

_____

_____

"But when you ask, you must believe and not doubt, because the one who doubts is like a wave of the sea, blown and tossed by the wind." ~ James 1:6

DATE: _____

PRAYER PROMPT – I'M RECLAIMING THIS…

_____

_____

_____

_____

_____

_____

_____

_____

_____

_____

_____

_____

_____

_____

_____

_____

"Therefore confess your sins to each other and pray for each other so that you may be healed. The prayer of a righteous person is powerful and effective."
~ James 5:16

_____

_____

_____

_____

_____

_____

_____

_____

_____

_____

_____

_____

_____

_____

_____

_____

_____

_____

_____

"Therefore confess your sins to each other and pray for each other so that you may be healed. The prayer of a righteous person is powerful and effective."
~ James 5:16

PRAYER PROMPT – THANK YOU LORD…

_____

_____

_____

_____

_____

_____

_____

_____

_____

_____

_____

_____

_____

_____

_____

_____

_____

"This is the confidence we have in approaching God: that if we ask anything according to His will, he hears us." ~ 1 John 5:14

"This is the confidence we have in approaching God: that if we ask anything according to His will, he hears us." ~ 1 John 5:14

DATE: _____

PRAYER PROMPT – I'M WAITING, LORD…

_____

_____

_____

_____

_____

_____

_____

_____

_____

_____

_____

_____

_____

_____

_____

_____

_____

_____

"And if we know that He hears us – whatever we ask – we know that we have what we asked of Him." ~ 1 John 5:15

_____

_____

_____

_____

_____

_____

_____

_____

_____

_____

_____

_____

_____

_____

_____

_____

_____

_____

_____

_____

"And if we know that He hears us – whatever we ask – we know that we have what we asked of Him." ~ 1 John 5:15

DATE: _____

PRAYER PROMPT – I'M TIRED, LORD…

_____

_____

_____

_____

_____

_____

_____

_____

_____

_____

_____

_____

_____

_____

_____

_____

"In the morning, Lord, you hear my voice; in the morning I lay my requests before you and wait expectantly." ~ Psalm 5:3

_____

_____

_____

_____

_____

_____

_____

_____

_____

_____

_____

_____

_____

_____

_____

_____

_____

_____

"In the morning, Lord, you hear my voice; in the morning I lay my requests before you and wait expectantly." ~ Psalm 5:3

DATE: _____

PRAYER PROMPT – MY SPOUSE/SIGNIFICANT OTHER…

_____

_____

_____

_____

_____

_____

_____

_____

_____

_____

_____

_____

_____

_____

_____

_____

_____

"If you believe, you will receive whatever you ask for in prayer." ~ Matthew 21:22

_____

_____

_____

_____

_____

_____

_____

_____

_____

_____

_____

_____

_____

_____

_____

_____

_____

_____

_____

_____

"If you believe, you will receive whatever you ask for in prayer." ~ Matthew 21:22

DATE: _____

PRAYER PROMPT – MY CHILDREN/GRANDCHILDREN…

_____

_____

_____

_____

_____

_____

_____

_____

_____

_____

_____

_____

_____

_____

_____

_____

_____

_____

_____

"The Lord will fight for you; you need only to be still." ~ Exodus 14:14

_____

_____

_____

_____

_____

_____

_____

_____

_____

_____

_____

_____

_____

_____

_____

_____

_____

_____

_____

_____

_____

_____

"The Lord will fight for you; you need only to be still." ~ Exodus 14:14

DATE: _____

PRAYER PROMPT – MY FAMILY AND FRIENDS…

_____

_____

_____

_____

_____

_____

_____

_____

_____

_____

_____

_____

_____

_____

_____

_____

_____

_____

_____

_____

"He says, "Be still, and know that I am God;"" ~ Psalm 46:10

_____

_____

_____

_____

_____

_____

_____

_____

_____

_____

_____

_____

_____

_____

_____

_____

_____

_____

_____

_____

_____

_____

"He says, "Be still, and know that I am God;"" ~ Psalm 46:10

DATE: _____

PRAYER PROMPT – COUNTING MY BLESSINGS…

_____

_____

_____

_____

_____

_____

_____

_____

_____

_____

_____

_____

_____

_____

_____

_____

_____

_____

_____

_____

"Cast all your anxiety on Him because He cares for you." ~ 1 Peter 5:7

_____

_____

_____

_____

_____

_____

_____

_____

_____

_____

_____

_____

_____

_____

_____

_____

_____

_____

_____

_____

_____

_____

_____

_____

"Cast all your anxiety on Him because He cares for you." ~ 1 Peter 5:7

DATE: _____

PRAYER PROMPT – I LOVE YOU, LORD…

_____

_____

_____

_____

_____

_____

_____

_____

_____

_____

_____

_____

_____

_____

_____

_____

_____

_____

"Ask and it will be given to you; seek and you will find; knock and the door will be opened to you." ~ Matthew 7:7

_____

_____

_____

_____

_____

_____

_____

_____

_____

_____

_____

_____

_____

_____

_____

_____

_____

_____

_____

_____

_____

_____

"Ask and it will be given to you; seek and you will find; knock and the door will be opened to you." ~ Matthew 7:7

DATE: _____

PRAYER PROMPT – IT'S BECAUSE OF YOU, LORD…

_____

_____

_____

_____

_____

_____

_____

_____

_____

_____

_____

_____

_____

_____

_____

_____

_____

_____

_____

"Humble yourselves before the Lord, and He will lift you up." ~ James 4:10

_____

_____

_____

_____

_____

_____

_____

_____

_____

_____

_____

_____

_____

_____

_____

_____

_____

_____

_____

_____

_____

"Humble yourselves before the Lord, and He will lift you up." ~ James 4:10

PRAYER PROMPT – MY ENEMIES AND MY FRENEMIES…

_____

_____

_____

_____

_____

_____

_____

_____

_____

_____

_____

_____

_____

_____

_____

_____

_____

_____

_____

"But to you who are listening I say: Love your enemies, do good to those who hate you, bless those who curse you, pray for those who mistreat you." ~ Luke 6:27-28

_____

_____

_____

_____

_____

_____

_____

_____

_____

_____

_____

_____

_____

_____

_____

_____

_____

_____

_____

"But to you who are listening I say: Love your enemies, do good to those who hate you, bless those who curse you, pray for those who mistreat you." ~ Luke 6:27-28

DATE: _____

PRAYER PROMPT – OPEN MY HEART…

_____

_____

_____

_____

_____

_____

_____

_____

_____

_____

_____

_____

_____

_____

_____

_____

_____

_____

_____

_____

"I can do all things through Him who gives me strength." ~ Philippians 4:13

_____

_____

_____

_____

_____

_____

_____

_____

_____

_____

_____

_____

_____

_____

_____

_____

_____

_____

_____

"I can do all things through Him who gives me strength." ~ Philippians 4:13

DATE: _____

PRAYER PROMPT – BUT GOD...

_____

_____

_____

_____

_____

_____

_____

_____

_____

_____

_____

_____

_____

_____

_____

_____

_____

_____

_____

"Wait for the Lord; be strong and take heart and wait for the Lord." ~ Psalm 27:14

_____

_____

_____

_____

_____

_____

_____

_____

_____

_____

_____

_____

_____

_____

_____

_____

_____

_____

_____

_____

_____

"Wait for the Lord; be strong and take heart and wait for the Lord." ~ Psalm 27:14

DATE: _____

PRAYER PROMPT – GRANT ME PATIENCE…

_____

_____

_____

_____

_____

_____

_____

_____

_____

_____

_____

_____

_____

_____

_____

_____

_____

_____

_____

_____

_____

"The Lord is my shepherd, I shall not want." ~ Psalm 23:1

_____

_____

_____

_____

_____

_____

_____

_____

_____

_____

_____

_____

_____

_____

_____

_____

_____

_____

_____

_____

"The Lord is my shepherd, I shall not want." ~ Psalm 23:1

DATE: _____

PRAYER PROMPT – GIVE ME THE COURAGE TO...

_____

_____

_____

_____

_____

_____

_____

_____

_____

_____

_____

_____

_____

_____

_____

_____

_____

_____

"The end of a matter is better than its beginning, and patience is better than pride." ~ Ecclesiastes 7:8

_____

_____

_____

_____

_____

_____

_____

_____

_____

_____

_____

_____

_____

_____

_____

_____

_____

_____

_____

_____

"The end of a matter is better than its beginning, and patience is better than pride." ~ Ecclesiastes 7:8

DATE: _____

PRAYER PROMPT – THIS UPCOMING PROJECT…

_____

_____

_____

_____

_____

_____

_____

_____

_____

_____

_____

_____

_____

_____

_____

_____

_____

_____

_____

_____

_____

"Commit your way to the Lord; trust in Him and he will do this." ~ Psalm 37:5

"Commit your way to the Lord; trust in Him and he will do this." ~ Psalm 37:5

DATE: _____

PRAYER PROMPT – GIVE ME WISDOM...

_____

_____

_____

_____

_____

_____

_____

_____

_____

_____

_____

_____

_____

_____

_____

_____

_____

"If any of you lacks wisdom, you should ask God, who gives generously to all without finding fault, and it will be given to you." ~ James 1:5

_____

_____

_____

_____

_____

_____

_____

_____

_____

_____

_____

_____

_____

_____

_____

_____

_____

_____

_____

_____

"If any of you lacks wisdom, you should ask God, who gives generously to all without finding fault, and it will be given to you." ~ James 1:5

DATE: _____

PRAYER PROMPT – GIVE ME DISCERNMENT…

_____

_____

_____

_____

_____

_____

_____

_____

_____

_____

_____

_____

_____

_____

_____

_____

_____

_____

_____

"So that you may be able to discern what is best and may be pure and blameless for the day of Christ," ~ Philippians 1:10

_____

_____

_____

_____

_____

_____

_____

_____

_____

_____

_____

_____

_____

_____

_____

_____

_____

_____

_____

"So that you may be able to discern what is best and may be pure and blameless for the day of Christ," ~ Philippians 1:10

DATE: _____

PRAYER PROMPT – IN MY SEASONS OF DOUBT…

_____

_____

_____

_____

_____

_____

_____

_____

_____

_____

_____

_____

_____

_____

_____

_____

_____

_____

_____

"Therefore encourage one another and build each other up, just as in fact you are doing." ~ 1 Thessalonians 5:11

_____

_____

_____

_____

_____

_____

_____

_____

_____

_____

_____

_____

_____

_____

_____

_____

_____

_____

_____

"Therefore encourage one another and build each other up, just as in fact you are doing." ~ 1 Thessalonians 5:11

DATE: _____

PRAYER PROMPT – ALL PRAISES DUE…

"But you Lord, are a shield around me." ~ Psalm 3:3

_____

_____

_____

_____

_____

_____

_____

_____

_____

_____

_____

_____

_____

_____

_____

_____

_____

_____

_____

_____

"But you Lord, are a shield around me." ~ Psalm 3:3

DATE: _____

PRAYER PROMPT – MY PURPOSE IN LIFE…

_____

_____

_____

_____

_____

_____

_____

_____

_____

_____

_____

_____

_____

_____

_____

_____

_____

_____

"And we know that in all things God works for the good of those who love him, who have been called according to his purpose." ~ Romans 8:28

_____

_____

_____

_____

_____

_____

_____

_____

_____

_____

_____

_____

_____

_____

_____

_____

_____

_____

_____

"And we know that in all things God works for the good of those who love him, who have been called according to his purpose." ~ Romans 8:28

DATE: _____

PRAYER PROMPT – TEACH ME TO TRUST YOU…

_____

_____

_____

_____

_____

_____

_____

_____

_____

_____

_____

_____

_____

_____

_____

_____

_____

_____

_____

_____

_____

"Trust in the Lord with all your heart and lean not on your understanding;"
~ Proverbs 3:5

_____

_____

_____

_____

_____

_____

_____

_____

_____

_____

_____

_____

_____

_____

_____

_____

_____

_____

_____

_____

"Trust in the Lord with all your heart and lean not on your understanding;"
~ Proverbs 3:5

PRAYER PROMPT – THE LEAST OF THESE…

"The King will reply, "Truly I tell you, whatever you did for one of the least of these brothers and sisters of mine, you did for me."" ~ Matthew 25:40

_____

_____

_____

_____

_____

_____

_____

_____

_____

_____

_____

_____

_____

_____

_____

_____

_____

_____

_____

"The King will reply, "Truly I tell you, whatever you did for one of the least of these brothers and sisters of mine, you did for me."" ~ Matthew 25:40

DATE: _____

PRAYER PROMPT – LEARNING TO BE CONTENT...

_____

_____

_____

_____

_____

_____

_____

_____

_____

_____

_____

_____

_____

_____

_____

_____

_____

_____

_____

_____

"Keep your lives free from the love of money and be content with what you have, because God has said, "Never will I leave you; never will I forsake you.""
~ Hebrews 13:5

_____

_____

_____

_____

_____

_____

_____

_____

_____

_____

_____

_____

_____

_____

_____

_____

_____

_____

_____

"Keep your lives free from the love of money and be content with what you have, because God has said, "Never will I leave you; never will I forsake you.""
~ Hebrews 13:5

DATE: _____

PRAYER PROMPT – I NEED HELP…

_____

_____

_____

_____

_____

_____

_____

_____

_____

_____

_____

_____

_____

_____

_____

_____

_____

_____

"I lift up my eyes to the mountains – where does my help come from? My help comes from the Lord, the Maker of heaven and earth." ~ Psalm 121:1-2

_____

_____

_____

_____

_____

_____

_____

_____

_____

_____

_____

_____

_____

_____

_____

_____

_____

_____

_____

"I lift up my eyes to the mountains – where does my help come from? My help comes from the Lord, the Maker of heaven and earth." ~ Psalm 121:1-2

PRAYER PROMPT – I'M SO DISCOURAGED RIGHT NOW...

_____

_____

_____

_____

_____

_____

_____

_____

_____

_____

_____

_____

_____

_____

_____

_____

_____

_____

_____

_____

"Have I not commanded you? Be strong and courageous. Do not be afraid; do not be discouraged, for the Lord your God will be with you wherever you go."
~ Joshua 1:9

_____

_____

_____

_____

_____

_____

_____

_____

_____

_____

_____

_____

_____

_____

_____

_____

_____

_____

_____

_____

"Have I not commanded you? Be strong and courageous. Do not be afraid; do not be discouraged, for the Lord your God will be with you wherever you go."
~ Joshua 1:9

DATE: _____

PRAYER PROMPT – OUR NATION/OUR WORLD…

_____

_____

_____

_____

_____

_____

_____

_____

_____

_____

_____

_____

_____

_____

_____

_____

_____

_____

_____

_____

"If my people, who are called by my name, will humble themselves and pray and seek my face and turn from their wicked ways, then I will hear from heaven, and I will forgive their sin and will heal their land." ~ 2 Chronicles 7:14

"If my people, who are called by my name, will humble themselves and pray and seek my face and turn from their wicked ways, then I will hear from heaven, and I will forgive their sin and will heal their land." ~ 2 Chronicles 7:14

DATE: _____

PRAYER PROMPT – FACING MY FEARS

_____

_____

_____

_____

_____

_____

_____

_____

_____

_____

_____

_____

_____

_____

_____

_____

_____

_____

"So do not fear, for I am with you; do not be dismayed, for I am your God. I will strengthen you and help you; I will uphold you with my righteous right hand." ~ Isaiah 41:10

_____

_____

_____

_____

_____

_____

_____

_____

_____

_____

_____

_____

_____

_____

_____

_____

_____

_____

"So do not fear, for I am with you; do not be dismayed, for I am your God. I will strengthen you and help you; I will uphold you with my righteous right hand." ~ Isaiah 41:10

DATE: _____

_____

_____

_____

_____

_____

_____

_____

_____

_____

_____

_____

_____

_____

_____

_____

_____

_____

_____

_____

"But thanks be to God! He gives us the victory through our Lord Jesus Christ!"
~ 1 Corinthians 15:57

_____

_____

_____

_____

_____

_____

_____

_____

_____

_____

_____

_____

_____

_____

_____

_____

_____

_____

_____

"But thanks be to God! He gives us the victory through our Lord Jesus Christ!"
~ 1 Corinthians 15:57

DATE: _____

PRAYER PROMPT – GIVE ME PEACE…

_____

_____

_____

_____

_____

_____

_____

_____

_____

_____

_____

_____

_____

_____

_____

_____

_____

_____

"I have told you these things, so that in me you may have peace. In this world you will have trouble. But take heart! I have overcome the world." ~ John 16:33

"I have told you these things, so that in me you may have peace. In this world you will have trouble. But take heart! I have overcome the world." ~ John 16:33

PRAYER PROMPT – MOMENTS OF TEMPTATION...

_____

_____

_____

_____

_____

_____

_____

_____

_____

_____

_____

_____

_____

_____

_____

_____

_____

"...and God is faithful; He will not let you be tempted beyond what you can bear." ~ 1 Corinthians 10:13

_____

_____

_____

_____

_____

_____

_____

_____

_____

_____

_____

_____

_____

_____

_____

_____

_____

_____

_____

_____

_____

"...and God is faithful; He will not let you be tempted beyond what you can bear." ~ 1 Corinthians 10:13

DATE: _____

PRAYER PROMPT – I SURRENDER ALL…

_____

_____

_____

_____

_____

_____

_____

_____

_____

_____

_____

_____

_____

_____

_____

_____

_____

_____

_____

"The thief comes only to steal and kill and destroy; I have come that they may have life, and have it to the full." ~ John 10:10

_____

_____

_____

_____

_____

_____

_____

_____

_____

_____

_____

_____

_____

_____

_____

_____

_____

_____

_____

_____

"The thief comes only to steal and kill and destroy; I have come that they may have life, and have it to the full." ~ John 10:10

PRAYER PROMPT – SO MANY ARE LOST…

_____

_____

_____

_____

_____

_____

_____

_____

_____

_____

_____

_____

_____

_____

_____

_____

_____

_____

"For the Son of man came to seek and to save the lost." ~ Luke 19:10

_____

_____

_____

_____

_____

_____

_____

_____

_____

_____

_____

_____

_____

_____

_____

_____

_____

_____

_____

_____

_____

"For the Son of man came to seek and to save the lost." ~ Luke 19:10

DATE: _____

_____

_____

_____

_____

_____

_____

_____

_____

_____

_____

_____

_____

_____

_____

_____

_____

_____

"Commit to the Lord whatever you do, and He will establish your plans."
~ Proverbs 16:3

_____

_____

_____

_____

_____

_____

_____

_____

_____

_____

_____

_____

_____

_____

_____

_____

_____

_____

_____

_____

_____

"Commit to the Lord whatever you do, and He will establish your plans."
~ Proverbs 16:3

DATE: _____

PRAYER PROMPT – I'M JUST A NOBODY…

_____

_____

_____

_____

_____

_____

_____

_____

_____

_____

_____

_____

_____

_____

_____

_____

"Teach me to do your will, for you are my God; may your good Spirit lead me on level ground." ~ Psalm 143:10

_____

_____

_____

_____

_____

_____

_____

_____

_____

_____

_____

_____

_____

_____

_____

_____

_____

_____

_____

_____

"Teach me to do your will, for you are my God; may your good Spirit lead me on level ground." ~ Psalm 143:10

DATE: _____

PRAYER PROMPT – ALL PRAISES DUE…

_____

_____

_____

_____

_____

_____

_____

_____

_____

_____

_____

_____

_____

_____

_____

_____

_____

_____

_____

_____

"I will extol the Lord at all times; His praise will always be on my lips." ~ Psalm 34:1

_____

_____

_____

_____

_____

_____

_____

_____

_____

_____

_____

_____

_____

_____

_____

_____

_____

_____

_____

"I will extol the Lord at all times; His praise will always be on my lips." ~ Psalm 34:1

DATE: _____

PRAYER PROMPT – DON'T GIVE UP…

_____

_____

_____

_____

_____

_____

_____

_____

_____

_____

_____

_____

_____

_____

_____

_____

_____

_____

_____

_____

"My grace is sufficient for you, for my power is made perfect in weakness."
~ 2 Corinthians 12:9

_____

_____

_____

_____

_____

_____

_____

_____

_____

_____

_____

_____

_____

_____

_____

_____

_____

_____

_____

_____

"My grace is sufficient for you, for my power is made perfect in weakness."
~ 2 Corinthians 12:9

DATE: _____

_____

_____

_____

_____

_____

_____

_____

_____

_____

_____

_____

_____

_____

_____

_____

_____

_____

_____

_____

_____

"It is more blessed to give than to receive." ~ Acts 20:35

"It is more blessed to give than to receive." ~ Acts 20:35

DATE: _____

PRAYER PROMPT – I NEED A RENEWAL...

_____

_____

_____

_____

_____

_____

_____

_____

_____

_____

_____

_____

_____

_____

_____

_____

_____

_____

_____

_____

"Create in me a pure heart, O God, and renew a steadfast spirit within me." ~ Psalm 51:10

_____

_____

_____

_____

_____

_____

_____

_____

_____

_____

_____

_____

_____

_____

_____

_____

_____

_____

_____

_____

_____

_____

"Create in me a pure heart, O God, and renew a steadfast spirit within me." ~ Psalm 51:10

DATE: _____

PRAYER PROMPT – I EXALT YOUR NAME…

_____

_____

_____

_____

_____

_____

_____

_____

_____

_____

_____

_____

_____

_____

_____

_____

_____

_____

"Lord, you are my God; I will exalt you and praise your name, for in perfect faithfulness you have done wonderful things, things planned long ago." ~ Isaiah 25:1

_____

_____

_____

_____

_____

_____

_____

_____

_____

_____

_____

_____

_____

_____

_____

_____

_____

_____

_____

_____

_____

_____

"Lord, you are my God; I will exalt you and praise your name, for in perfect faithfulness you have done wonderful things, things planned long ago." ~ Isaiah 25:1

DATE: _____

PRAYER PROMPT – HAVE MERCY ON ME…

_____

_____

_____

_____

_____

_____

_____

_____

_____

_____

_____

_____

_____

_____

_____

_____

_____

_____

_____

_____

_____

"Have mercy on me, O God, according to your unfailing love…"~ Psalm 51:1

_____

_____

_____

_____

_____

_____

_____

_____

_____

_____

_____

_____

_____

_____

_____

_____

_____

_____

_____

_____

_____

"Have mercy on me, O God, according to your unfailing love…"~ Psalm 51:1

PRAYER PROMPT – IT'S A NEW DAY...

_____

_____

_____

_____

_____

_____

_____

_____

_____

_____

_____

_____

_____

_____

_____

_____

_____

_____

"Therefore do not lose heart. Though outwardly we are wasting away, yet inwardly we are being renewed day by day." ~ 2 Corinthians 4:16

_____

_____

_____

_____

_____

_____

_____

_____

_____

_____

_____

_____

_____

_____

_____

_____

_____

_____

_____

"Therefore do not lose heart. Though outwardly we are wasting away, yet inwardly we are being renewed day by day." ~ 2 Corinthians 4:16

PRAYER PROMPT – HELP ME FORGIVE MYSELF…

_____

_____

_____

_____

_____

_____

_____

_____

_____

_____

_____

_____

_____

_____

_____

_____

_____

_____

_____

"Forgive as the Lord forgave you." ~ Colossians 3:13

"Forgive as the Lord forgave you." ~ Colossians 3:13

DATE: _____

PRAYER PROMPT – I ALMOST LET GO...

_____

_____

_____

_____

_____

_____

_____

_____

_____

_____

_____

_____

_____

_____

_____

_____

_____

"God is our refuge and strength, an ever-present help in trouble." ~ Psalm 46:1

_____

_____

_____

_____

_____

_____

_____

_____

_____

_____

_____

_____

_____

_____

_____

_____

_____

_____

_____

_____

"God is our refuge and strength, an ever-present help in trouble." ~ Psalm 46:1

DATE: _____

PRAYER PROMPT – IS MY LIGHT SHINING?

_____

_____

_____

_____

_____

_____

_____

_____

_____

_____

_____

_____

_____

_____

_____

_____

_____

_____

_____

"In the same way, let your light shine before others, that they may see your good deeds and glorify your Father in heaven." ~ Matthew 5:16

_____

_____

_____

_____

_____

_____

_____

_____

_____

_____

_____

_____

_____

_____

_____

_____

_____

_____

_____

"In the same way, let your light shine before others, that they may see your good deeds and glorify your Father in heaven." ~ Matthew 5:16

PRAYER PROMPT – MY CUP HAS OVERFLOWED...

_____

_____

_____

_____

_____

_____

_____

_____

_____

_____

_____

_____

_____

_____

_____

_____

_____

_____

"But blessed is the one who trusts in the Lord, whose confidence is in him."
~ Jeremiah 17:7

_____

_____

_____

_____

_____

_____

_____

_____

_____

_____

_____

_____

_____

_____

_____

_____

_____

_____

_____

_____

"But blessed is the one who trusts in the Lord, whose confidence is in him."
~ Jeremiah 17:7

PRAYER PROMPT – AM I A HYPOCRITE?

_____

_____

_____

_____

_____

_____

_____

_____

_____

_____

_____

_____

_____

_____

_____

_____

_____

_____

"How can you say to your brother, 'Brother, let me take the speck out of your eye,' when you yourself fail to see the plank in your own eye?" ~ Luke 6:42

_____

_____

_____

_____

_____

_____

_____

_____

_____

_____

_____

_____

_____

_____

_____

_____

_____

_____

_____

_____

_____

"How can you say to your brother, 'Brother, let me take the speck out of your eye,' when you yourself fail to see the plank in your own eye?" ~ Luke 6:42

PRAYER PROMPT – STARTING OVER…

_____

_____

_____

_____

_____

_____

_____

_____

_____

_____

_____

_____

_____

_____

_____

_____

_____

_____

_____

"Because of the Lord's great love we are not consumed, for his compassions never fail. They are new every morning; great is your faithfulness." ~ Lamentations 3:22-23

_____

_____

_____

_____

_____

_____

_____

_____

_____

_____

_____

_____

_____

_____

_____

_____

_____

_____

_____

_____

_____

"Because of the Lord's great love we are not consumed, for his compassions never fail. They are new every morning; great is your faithfulness." ~ Lamentations 3:22-23

DATE: _____

PRAYER PROMPT – WHY ME, LORD?

_____

_____

_____

_____

_____

_____

_____

_____

_____

_____

_____

_____

_____

_____

_____

_____

_____

_____

"My God, my God, why have you forsaken me? Why are you so far from saving me, so far from my cries of anguish?" ~ Psalm 22:1

_____

_____

_____

_____

_____

_____

_____

_____

_____

_____

_____

_____

_____

_____

_____

_____

_____

_____

_____

"My God, my God, why have you forsaken me? Why are you so far from saving me, so far from my cries of anguish?" ~ Psalm 22:1

DATE: _____

_____

_____

_____

_____

_____

_____

_____

_____

_____

_____

_____

_____

_____

_____

_____

_____

_____

_____

"If you remain in me and my words remain in you, ask whatever you wish and it will be done for you." ~ John 15:7

_____

_____

_____

_____

_____

_____

_____

_____

_____

_____

_____

_____

_____

_____

_____

_____

_____

_____

_____

_____

_____

"My God, my God, why have you forsaken me? Why are you so far from saving me, so far from my cries of anguish?" ~ Psalm 22:1

NOTES

NOTES

NOTES

NOTES

NOTES

NOTES

NOTES

www.ingramcontent.com/pod-product-compliance
Lightning Source LLC
Chambersburg PA
CBHW061733020426
42331CB00006B/1219